fast fun & easy

Incredible
Thread-A-Bowls
2 Techniques—5 Projects—
Unlimited Possibilities

Wendy Hill

C&T PUBLISHING

Text © 2005 Wendy Hill

Artwork © 2005 C&T Publishing, Inc.

Publisher: Amy Marson

Editorial Director: Gailen Runge

Acquisitions Editor: Jan Grigsby

Editor: Lynn Koolish

Technical Editors: Rene J. Steinpress and Wendy Mathson

Copyeditor/Proofreader: Wordfirm, Inc.

Cover Designer: Christina Jarumay

Production Artist/Illustrator: Kirstie L. Pettersen

Production Assistant: Matt Allen

Photography: Luke Mulks and Diane Pedersen

Published by C&T Publishing, Inc., P.O. Box 1456, Lafayette, CA 94549

Library of Congress Cataloging-in-Publication Data

Hill, Wendy,

Fast, fun & easy incredible thread-a-bowls: 2 techniques, 5 projects, unlimited possibilities / Wendy Hill.

p. cm.

ISBN 1-57120-331-1 (paper trade)

1. Textile crafts. 2. Machine sewing. 3. Bowls (Tableware) 4. Thread. 5. Stabilizing agents. I. Title: Fast, fun and easy incredible thread-a-bowls. II. Title.

TT715.H55 2005

746—dc22

2005013130

Printed in China

10 9 8 7 6 5 4 3 2 1

Dedication

For David and Lucas

merrily, merrily, merrily, merrily . . .

Acknowledgments

The saying "It takes a village to raise a child" applies equally well to the writing and publishing of a book. A simple idea grows and takes shape until the book reaches a gawky stage and starts to talk back. With the help of family and friends and the team at C&T, the book grows up and matures, ready to take its place on bookshelves.

For all of you who helped me raise a book from idea to a published volume, thank you. Thank you, Karla Rogers, for invaluable help with turning a phrase and making the hard but necessary changes, and everything else. Thank you, Chris Shaker, for suggesting a shopping trip to a fly-fishing supply store; I never would have thought of this on my own. Thank you, Jane Croley, Joan Metzger, Sue McMahan, Kathy Shaker, and Carol Web, for your continuous support, encouragement, and inspiration. Thank you, Christine and Paul Drumright, April and Bob Hill, Sue McMahan, and Kathy and Chris Shaker, for letting me temporarily take back "my" bowls for use in this book. Thank you, Susan Howell and Kathy Shaker, for testing my directions with your own thread-web creations. Thank you, Lynn, my editor, for the loan of the thread-web scarf and so much more! Thank you to everyone else at C&T Publishing for all the things you do, both seen and unseen.

A big thank you to the following companies, which generously donated products for use in this book. Please see Resources (page 48) for more information about these companies and their products.

American & Efird (Mettler, Signature Thread)

Coats & Clark

Gütermann of America, Inc.

Huckleberry Quiltworks, Inc. (Aurifil, Aurilux Thread)

Madeira SCS/USA

Sulky of America

YLI Corporation

Contents

Introduction

I love thread the way most quilters love fabric. Fabric stash? I don't have one. Thread stash? You bet! I'll buy thread for any reason or no reason at all.

About fifteen years ago, I started using thread to create texture on fabric. I quickly used up my box of leftover thread spools, but it was too late. I was hooked. Using a regular straight stitch, with the feed dogs engaged (*not* free-motion), I found a way to embellish fabric with crisscrossed stitching lines—a technique I call "surface stitching."

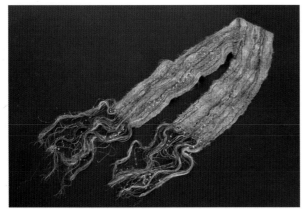

Thread-web scarf by Lynn Koolish

Wendy's first thread-web bowl

Thread-web containers

The new water-soluble stabilizer products, marketed for machine embroidery, opened up doors for more experimentation. Like others around the globe, I started using this stabilizer to sandwich fibers together so I could stitch through it all with a crisscrossed web of stitching lines. I then washed out the stabilizer, leaving a pliable stitched thread-web that I could use to create scarves, vest or jacket fronts, new fabric, and so on.

But what happens when the water-soluble stabilizer isn't completely washed out? I discovered the answer by accident when my thread-web dried as stiff as a board. While grumbling about having to wash it again, some other part of my mind asked "what if" questions about dried, stiff thread-webs. I immediately dropped everything to make my first thread-web bowl.

When an invisible but sticky residue of the stabilizer is left behind, it dries stiff. This stiffness allows you to make three-dimensional containers out of practically nothing, such as thread, fabric snips, and other fun filler materials. These thread-web containers can be impossibly delicate and light, like gossamer, or incredibly dense, like handblown glass or pottery.

In this book are five projects and many variations, the result of my almost ten years of experimentation and problem solving with thread-web containers. Amaze your family and friends with your own intricate and seemingly impossible thread-web vases, cups, and bowls—just don't reveal how easy it is!

getting started

Making a thread-web bowl is a fun and forgiving process. This is a good time to experiment with a variety of materials, thread types, and stitch styles, including free-motion stitching.

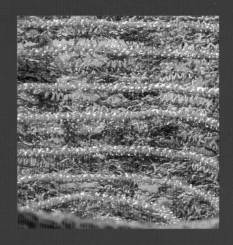

Collect the Supplies

All thread-web vases, cups, and bowls start with water-soluble stabilizer, filler materials (if you like), and stitching. You sandwich the filler materials (thread, yarns, other fiber-like things) between two layers of stabilizer and machine stitch. After you rinse out most, but not all, of the water-soluble stabilizer, the thread-web container dries stiff. It is then ready to be permanently sealed with an acrylic spray finish.

Individual stitching lines that stand out while you're stitching blend in by the time the bowl is finished. Any problems with color choices or stitch quality vanish once you wash out the stabilizer. With thread-webs, there are no mistakes—only happy accidents!

filler materials

Thread-web containers are all about color and texture, the two things we love about working with fiber and fabric. Look for materials that are sewable and washable. I would say that anything goes, but I have discovered it is impossible to get good stitch quality sewing through balloons!

Thread

Thread makes a wonderful filler material and is readily accessible. You can use thread right off the spools or leftover bobbins.

Threads for filler

fast!

Save those thread snips! Keep a bag next to your sewing machine for all your thread snips as you sew. You'll have enough for a thread-web bowl in no time!

Thread snips

Raveled Fabric Edges

Prewashing fabric will never be the same. As the fabric comes out of the washer, inspect the cut edges for the balled up raveled fibers. Cut these off and save for future thread-web projects. Being thrifty never felt so good!

Raveled fibers

Fabric Snips

Save even the smallest scrap of reversible and hand-dyed fabrics. Cut the scraps into snips (random shapes, squares, triangles), and toss them into the mix of filler materials for your next thread-web project.

Fabric scraps

Novelty Fabrics

Look at novelty fabrics with a new purpose in mind. Fabrics with smaller motifs, such as flowers, fruit, animals, aliens, and so on, make a great filler material for thread-web bowls. You can cluster or scatter the cutout motifs with the other filler material.

Novelty fabrics

Yarns, Perle Cotton, and Chenille

Look for yarns, perle cotton, and chenille in craft, yarn, and some fabric shops. Ask your knitting friends or friendly shop owners to save leftover yarn bits for you. Start collecting now so you'll have a stash when you want to make your next thread-web bowl.

Yarns, perle cotton, and chenille

Ribbons, Trims, and Floss

More and more stores now carry ribbons, trims, and fibers of all sorts. In addition to craft and fabric shops, check out papermaking and scrapbooking stores. You never know what you might find!

Ribbons, trims, and fibers

Artificial Flowers

Artificial silk flowers are a fantastic source of color and texture, and they are often on sale at the end of a season. Dismantle and save the fabric leaves and flower petals to use whole or cut into smaller pieces.

Artificial flowers

The Hunt for Fun Stuff

Keep an eye out for fun and exciting filler materials by expanding the hunt beyond your usual quilt shopping spots. I already mentioned papermaking and scrapbooking stores, but what about hardware stores, yarn shops, stationery stores, or even fly-fishing supply stores. Among the supplies to make flies for fishing are wonderful filler materials, including synthetic and metallic fluff and strands, chenille yarns, and braided cords in fun fish- (and human-) appealing colors. If you can sew through and wash it, it's fair game for a thread-web bowl.

Fun stuff

water-soluble stabilizer

Water-soluble stabilizer is a nontoxic, environmentally friendly, biodegradable material that is designed to dissolve in water. There are many brands available, but I recommend Sulky Super Solvy and Sulky Ultra Solvy.

Be sure to store all water-soluble stabilizers in plastic bags or boxes so they don't get dried out and brittle.

Water-soluble stabilizer

fast!

Here are 3 ways to make Solvy adhesive as an alternative to pinning the layers.

☐ Tape a piece of Ultra Solvy to the work surface. Moisten the Solvy with a damp sponge. Layer the filler, then cover with a piece of Super Solvy. Press the sandwich together and let dry before sewing.

☐ Rub a glue stick vertically and horizontally across a piece of Super Solvy. Layer the filler, then cover with another piece of Super Solvy. Press them together and let dry before sewing.

☐ When the filler is sparse, with gaps where the Solvy layers touch, use a press cloth and a steam setting on your iron to press the Solvy sandwich. Check to make sure the sandwich is sticking together. Don't overheat or it will become brittle or melt.

forms for molding

When looking for shapes and forms for molding your thread-web containers, remember it is the shape that counts, not the beauty of the form itself. Rummage through your cupboards for interesting and suitable bowls, vases, cups, dishes, and shallow platters.

The forms shown here have the "right" kind of shape: vertical or narrow at the bottom and wider at the top. This shape allows the loosened dried thread-web to slide right off.

Forms with the right shape

Forms do not have to be round to qualify for a thread-web project. As long as the form is vertical or narrow at the bottom and wider at the top, any shape will work. Unusual shapes make interesting thread-web vases, cups, and bowls!

These forms also work well.

Consider forms with texture or bulges, but remember the thread-web is usually too delicate to pick up these features unless they are exaggerated. Look at the bowls below. After being molded on the bubbly textured vase, the dried thread-web will appear smooth, not bubbly. However, the thread-web could be pushed into the holes of the washer bowl for a lot of physical texture.

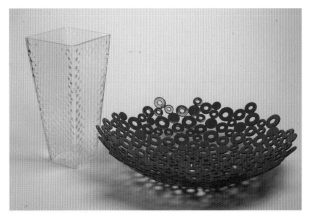

Subtle textures won't show up on thread-web bowls, but openings provide opportunities to create texture.

The green bowl has shallow, rounded tiers, while the blue bowl has deep, angular tiers. A thread-web bowl made on the green form will have a subtle shape as compared with a thread-web bowl made on the blue bowl.

Shapes that are more distinct transfer better.

Take a second look at possible forms before discarding them. At first glance, this vase and big jug may seem inappropriate because the dried thread-web can't slide off. But both could be used to make shallow bowls, molded on the bottom only.

Consider different ways to use a form before eliminating it as a possibility.

At first glance, this fluted vase may seem impossible, because of all the nooks and crannies. But it *is* narrow at the bottom and wider at the top. In addition, if the thread-web is delicate enough, it can be pressed into the hollows for an interesting shape.

If the dried thread-web will slide off the form, it can be used, no matter how convoluted the form is.

Forms that are wide at the bottom and narrower at the top pose a problem: How do you get the dried thread-web off the form? Avoiding these forms still leaves plenty of others to choose from. However, the challenge of using these forms might be appealing (see Oddly Shaped Molds on pages 46–47).

Forms with the "wrong" shape

thread for machine stitching

The stabilizer sandwich is held together with criss-crossed lines of stitching. Use any good-quality thread.

Variegated threads are fun and easy to use—you get a lot of color from one thread. They can be found in cotton, rayon, polyester, and even metallic, so try any of them. Look for different weights and finishes to add to the overall look of your thread-web bowl. Using thick or thin threads with dull or shiny surfaces changes the look of the finished thread-web.

easy!

If in serious doubt about a thread or decorative stitch choice, do a test-drive along the edge of the water-soluble stabilizer sandwich. Trim off any test runs before finishing the thread-web container.

Thread-web bowls are a great way to try out new threads. Just make sure you match the thread to the needle type: embroidery needles for embroidery or other fine threads; top-stitch needles for heavier-weight thread; metallic needles for metallic, holographic, and Sliver threads; and microtex sharps or universal needles for just about everything else.

Thread-web bowls are also a great place to practice your free-motion stitching. The threads cross so many times, any problems with stitch length or quality disappear when you rinse out the stabilizer.

Threads for machine stitching

fun!

If you have threads that are too thick to go through the needle, try winding them onto the bobbin. Sew with the right side facing down, so the bobbin thread stitches out on the right side of the stabilizer. These two bowls use bobbin quilting with decorative threads.

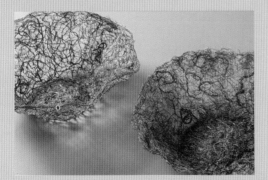

Sea Sparkles With Aqua Edge and *Wandering Ribbons With Pink Edge*, made by Elizabeth Hendricks

fast!

Use a water-soluble thread, such as YLI Washaway, to sew together leftover pieces of water-soluble stabilizer into one big piece. The thread melts away in warm water when you rinse out the stabilizer.

basic sewing supplies

Of course, you'll need to stock up on sewing machine needles of all sorts and sizes so you can match the needle to the thread. In addition to the other usual basics, you'll need a walking foot, a darning foot (if you want to do free-motion stitching), a rotary cutter and mat, and scissors for cutting paper and fabric.

Pins, walking foot, darning foot, rotary cutter and mat, scissors

odds and ends

The finished, dried thread-web container will pick up moisture from the air and deflate unless sealed with an **acrylic spray finish.** I use Krylon UV-Resistant Clear acrylic coating, but any equivalent spray will work. Be sure to follow the manufacturer's instructions, and always use the spray outdoors or in a well-ventilated room.

Newsprint is the perfect weight for making paper templates. Buy a pad of newsprint at a craft or office supply store. For an economical supply of newsprint, check your local newspaper for free or inexpensive roll ends of newsprint. If you want to try using regular printed newspaper, test it first to make sure the ink doesn't smear and transfer to your thread-web.

Look for **Reynolds Parchment Paper** in your grocery store right next to the Reynolds Freezer Wrap. Use a piece of parchment paper to keep the bowls from sticking to the counter and your hands when you are placing the wet thread-web over the form. You can use this durable, nonsticky paper over and over.

Thread-webs dried over a form are temporarily stuck to the mold. A little careful prying with a **wooden skewer** or something similar will help release the web from the mold.

Odds and ends: Parchment paper, newsprint, acrylic spray finish, wooden skewers

Take Care of Your Best Friend

I'm talking about taking care of your sewing machine, not taking your quilting buddy out to lunch. With other projects, actual sewing is intermittent while you pin, press, or cut more fabrics. Stitching a thread-web is nonstop sewing until the bobbin runs out or you change thread spools. Your machine can handle the work if you give it some help.

You'll need to do all the routine things—only do them more often. With each bobbin change, clean out the lint from under the throat plate and inside the hook race. With every other bobbin change, clean and oil your machine. After hours of continuous sewing, the point on the needle is no longer a point—get in the habit of changing the needle every three to four hours of sewing time.

basic supplies for each project

For each project in this book, you'll need the following basic supplies, some of which are described above in more detail:

☐ Measuring tape

☐ Compass or circular object to trace around

☐ Rotary cutter, cutting mat, and grid ruler

☐ Scissors

☐ Newsprint

☐ Appropriate sewing machine feet: walking foot, regular foot, optional darning foot for free-motion

☐ Parchment paper

☐ Wooden skewer

☐ UV-resistant clear acrylic spray

bowl basics

All thread-web bowls follow similar basic steps. Just like a spider weaves a web with an underlying structure, you'll start your thread-web with an underlying grid. Additional stitching crisscrosses the grid; the more the thread lines cross, the more stable the finished thread-web will be.

Make a Molded Thread-Web Bowl

A molded thread-web bowl starts out as a flat, stitched, water-soluble stabilizer sandwich. After rinsing out most of the stabilizer material, press the thread-web onto a form and allow it to dry.

The following step-by-step photo guide shows, in detail, how to make a molded bowl with a firm rim from start to finish. Use this guide as a reference when making your own projects.

1. measure the form   Measure the bowl or form from rim to rim. Be sure to measure over the center of the bottom of the form.

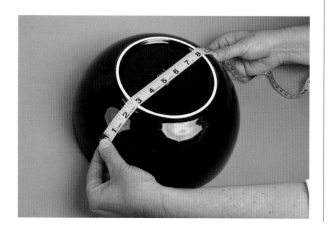

For a smaller thread-web bowl that retains the bottom shape of the form, start and end the measurement at any point from side to side.

2. make the template and cut the stabilizer   To make the paper template, use the measurement from Step 1 as the diameter of the circle, and draw the circle with a compass or trace around the rim of a plate or bowl that has the same diameter. Cut 2 square pieces of water-soluble stabilizer about 2˝ larger than the template.

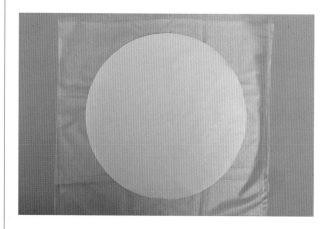

3. prepare the filler   Prepare all the filler materials now. Cut thread, make fabric snips, and so on, so everything will be ready to pile on the stabilizer. (See pages 6–8 for more filler material ideas.)

4. create the stabilizer sandwich

Center a piece of the water-soluble stabilizer over the paper template. Use the template as a placement guide and distribute the filler materials on the stabilizer so that the filler extends past the template edges. Cover with the second piece of stabilizer.

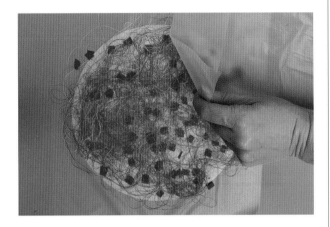

5. secure the sandwich
Carefully slide the stabilizer sandwich off the paper template. Secure the sandwich with pins, placed in columns for easy sewing. (See tip on page 8 for other ways to secure the sandwich.)

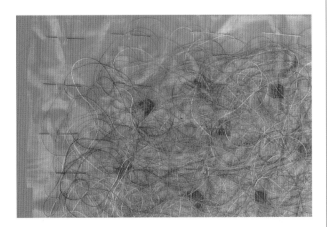

6. stitch a grid
Use a walking foot to stitch the first grid lines 1″ to 2″ apart, removing the pins as you sew.

Continue to use the walking foot to finish stitching the underlying grid. Sew vertically, horizontally, diagonally in one direction, and then diagonally in the other direction, using one or a variety of thread colors and types.

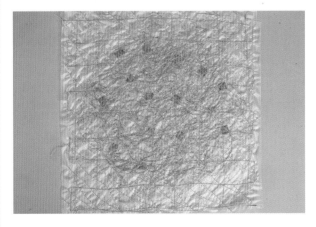

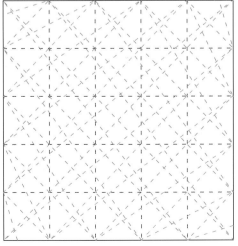

Underlying stitching grid

7. add more stitching

Change to a regular sewing foot if desired, and stitch some more. The more the stitching lines cross, the better, so keep sewing at all angles or around and around from the rim to the center and back again. If you prefer, free-motion stitch by dropping the feed dogs and using a darning foot. Continue to change thread type and color as it suits you.

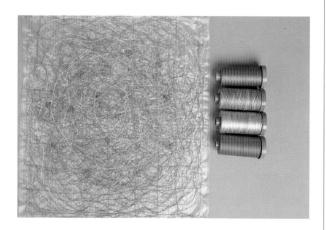

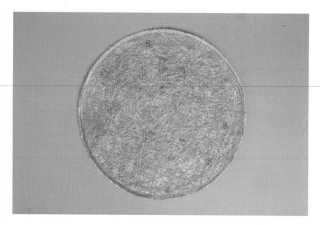

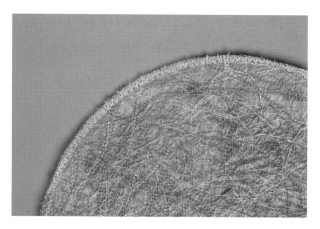

8. cut to size

Center and pin the paper template to the stitched water-soluble stabilizer sandwich. Cut out.

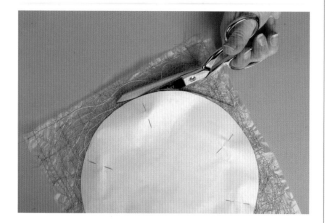

Leave the rim as is for a moderately firm rim, or reinforce the cut edge with stitching for a very firm rim. Use a zigzag stitch, satin stitch, serge stitch, multiple rounds of straight stitching, or a combination of stitch styles. (See page 45 for more rim options.)

9. dissolve the stabilizer

Set up a work area near a sink. To protect the work surface, spread out a piece of parchment paper larger than the form. Hold the stabilizer sandwich under warm, running water until the sandwich is soaked and sticky. Gently press or squeeze out the excess water until the thread-web glistens like a soap bubble and feels sticky.

10. mold the thread-web

Open the thread-web, and place it on the form, pressing it in place. If your thread-web has a "right side" (a side you like best), think about whether you want the preferred side on the inside or the outside of your finished container. Once the thread-web is pressed into place, allow it to dry completely.

easy!

If your hands stick to the wet thread-web as you mold it, wet your hands or use a wet piece of parchment paper to press the thread-web into place.

11. remove the dried thread-web

After the thread-web is completely dry, gently loosen the web from the form using a wooden skewer or something similar. Continue to loosen the web until it lifts off the form. Be patient; it will come off in no time.

12. seal the finished bowl

Seal your dried thread-web bowl with acrylic spray. Be sure to follow the manufacturer's instructions, and always use the spray outside or in a well-ventilated room. Instead of one heavy coat, spray several light coats on each side of the bowl, allowing drying time between each coat.

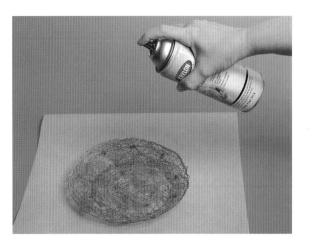

easy!

Shiny areas that remain after your thread-web bowl is dry indicate that a thin film of dried water-soluble stabilizer was left behind during the rinsing process. You can try to get rid of these areas in one of two ways. First, try blotting out the spot with a damp paper towel or a damp, soft rag. Let the thread-web dry again. The second solution calls for rinsing out the thread-web again, then reshaping or remolding it, and allowing it to dry. Or, you could just ignore the shiny spots altogether.

Make a Shaped Thread-Web Bowl

A shaped container starts out as a flat, stitched stabilizer sandwich, but you shape and stitch it into a bowl before rinsing out the stabilizer. Most shaped bowls still need some support while drying until they are dry enough to hold their shape. When completely dry, the shaped container is ready for you to seal and use.

The following step-by-step photo guide shows, in detail, how to make a shaped bowl with a wild rim from start to finish. Use this guide as a reference when making your own projects.

1. **make the template and cut the stabilizer**   To make the template, use a compass or trace around found objects to draw a circle on paper. The template will determine the size of the finished container after it is shaped. Add a smaller inner circle in the center of the large circle. The inner circle defines the bottom of the bowl, while the distance between the inner circle and the outer circle becomes the sides of the bowl. Cut 2 square pieces of water-soluble stabilizer about 2″ larger than the finished circle template.

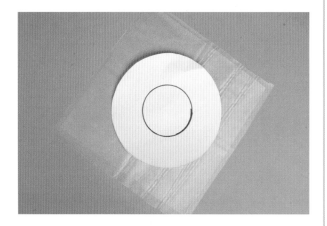

2. **mark the cutting lines**   Fold the circle template 4 times to make 8 equal divisions (vertically, horizontally, diagonally in one direction, and diagonally in the other direction). Draw a line from the rim to the inner circle along each fold line. These are the cutting lines for the slits needed to shape the bowl.

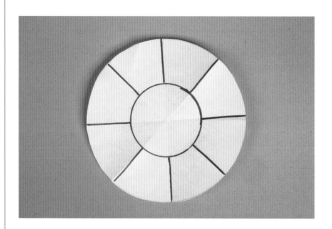

3. **prepare the filler**   Prepare all the filler materials now. Cut thread, make fabric snips, and so on, so everything will be ready to pile on the stabilizer. (See pages 6–8 for more filler material ideas.)

easy!

To make sure the template circles are centered, draw the first circle. Then fold the cutting lines (Step 2). Mark the center point and center the inner circle.

4. create the stabilizer sandwich

Center a piece of the water-soluble stabilizer over the paper template. Use the template as a placement guide and distribute the filler materials on the stabilizer so that the filler extends past the template edges. Cover with the second piece of stabilizer.

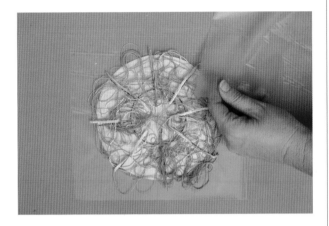

5. secure the sandwich
Carefully slide the stabilizer sandwich off the paper template. Secure the sandwich with pins, placed in columns for easy sewing. (See tip on page 8 for other ways to secure the sandwich.)

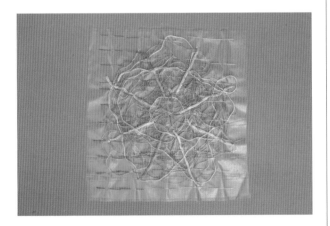

6. stitch a grid
Use a walking foot to stitch the first grid lines 1″ to 2″ apart, removing the pins as you sew.

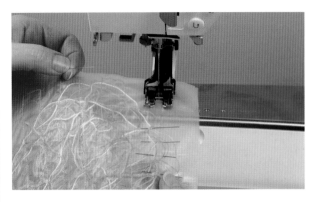

Continue to use the walking foot to finish stitching the underlying grid. Sew vertically, horizontally, diagonally in one direction, and then diagonally in the other direction, using one or a variety of thread colors and types.

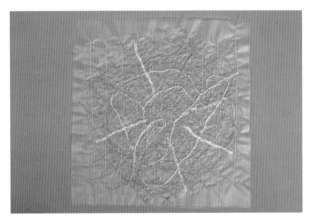

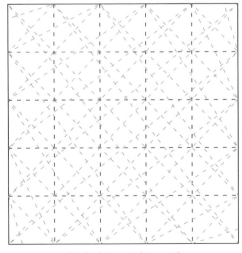

Underlying stitching grid

7. add more stitching Change to a regular sewing foot if desired, and stitch some more. The more the stitching lines cross, the better, so keep sewing at all angles or around and around from the rim to the center and back again. If you prefer, free-motion stitch by dropping the feed dogs and using a darning foot. Continue to change thread type and color as it suits you, keeping in mind that you will add more stitching after shaping the bowl (see Step 9).

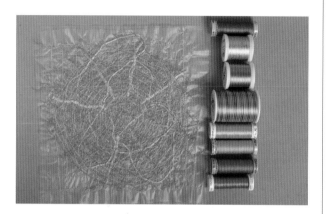

8. cut to size Center and pin the paper template to the stitched water-soluble stabilizer sandwich. For a wild rim (as shown), start at the outside edge of the stabilizer sandwich, and cut only along the marked slit lines. Trim the square corners of the stabilizer sandwich if desired, but leave a good inch of sandwich beyond the edge of the template. Remove the paper template after cutting and trimming.

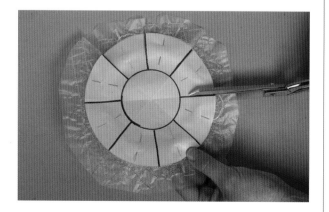

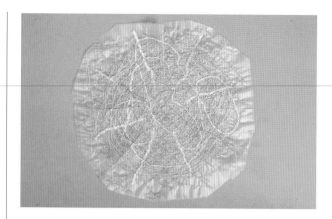

9. shape the bowl Overlap the cut edges of the slits, and pin in place. The more the edges overlap, the more steeply the sides of the bowl will come up. Sew along the cut edges of the slits.

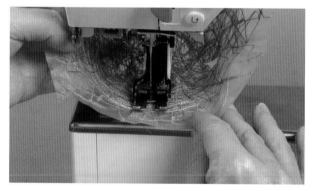

Add more stitching around the bowl to secure the cut edges, leaving the excess stabilizer around the outer edge unstitched, so the threads can go wild in the drying process. For example, stitch from the rim to the center of the bowl with thick thread, using a denim or triple stitch, a bright color, or a blending thread color.

10. dissolve the stabilizer

Set up a work area near a sink. To protect the work surface, spread out a piece of parchment paper larger than the bowl. Hold the thread-web under warm, running water until the thread-web is soaked and sticky. Gently press or squeeze out the excess water until the thread-web glistens like a soap bubble and feels sticky.

11. let the shaped bowl dry

Usually a shaped bowl will need some initial support while drying until it can stand on its own. Try setting the thread-web bowl right side up with a weight on the bottom of the bowl. Tug on the sides to position the sides of the bowl.

If the sides sag, place the bowl upside down over an object until it is stiff enough to continue drying right side up. It's okay to fiddle with the thread-web while it dries to get the shape you want.

12. seal the finished bowl

Seal your dried thread-web bowl with acrylic spray. Be sure to follow the manufacturer's instructions, and always use the spray outside or in a well-ventilated room. Instead of one heavy coat, spray several light coats on each side of the bowl, allowing drying time between coats.

fast!

If you don't like the shape of your thread-web bowl and it's unsealed, you can reshape the dried thread-web. Just wet it and squeeze out the excess water. Reshape or remold the bowl, let it dry, and seal. (My cute little kitty took a nap in one of my damp thread-web bowls! Needless to say, I had to reshape the bowl.)

square bowl

Take advantage of seasonal products to make themed thread-web containers to decorate your home. Use fall colors and metallic accents, as shown in this project, or substitute another seasonal or holiday color scheme for your project. Almost any shape of form will work if you can't find a square bowl.

What You'll Need

- Square (or other shape) form for molding
- Water-soluble stabilizer, 2 square pieces about 2″ larger than the diameter of your template
- Assorted filler materials: variegated thread, embroidery floss, perle cotton, and optional lightweight metallic shapes and garland
- Assorted spools of thread for sewing
- Basic supplies (see page 12)

How-Tos

Refer to the corresponding steps in Make a Molded Thread-Web Bowl (pages 14–17).

1. **measure the form** When using a square (or triangle) bowl, measure from rim to rim across the bottom of the form.

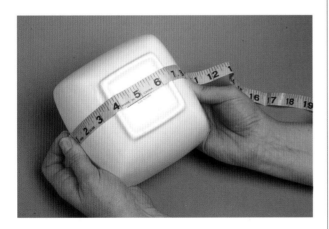

2. **make the template and cut the stabilizer**

To make the paper template, use the measurement from Step 1 as the diameter of the circle. Cut 2 square pieces of water-soluble stabilizer about 2″ larger than the template.

3. **prepare the filler**

4. **create the stabilizer sandwich**

easy!

When using small bits of chopped filler materials, trap the bits between two layers of thread. First unwind some thread onto the stabilizer. Sprinkle the bits over the surface. Then unwind some more thread on top. Cover with the second piece of stabilizer.

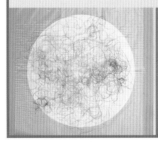 

5. **secure the sandwich**

6. **stitch a grid**

7. add more stitching
The density of the thread-web should be medium-light to light, so that it will fold in on itself when molded over the square bowl. (See page 44 for more information about density.)

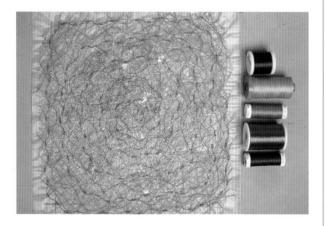

easy!

Don't worry about pleats and tucks that might get stitched into the water-soluble stabilizer. The water-soluble stabilizer is not a permanent part of your bowl. All the pleats and tucks will wash out with the stabilizer.

8. cut to size

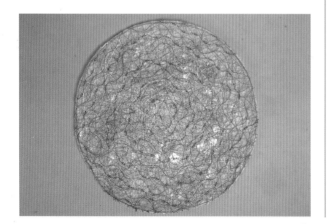

9. dissolve the stabilizer

10. mold the thread-web
Open the thread-web, and place it right side down on the form, pressing it in place. Use wet hands or a small piece of wet parchment paper to press the sticky web against the form.

11. remove the dried thread-web

12. seal the finished bowl

13. optional garland embellishment
Embellish the rim with a foil garland for a festive look. Cut the garland into 4 sections, long enough to overlap at the corners. Bend about ¼″ of the garland at each end, so it will wrap around to the next side. Whipstitch in place at both ends with a blending colored thread or floss.

Variations

A. The filler materials include raveled fabric edges. These thread-web bowls sit on three little knobs, or feet, picked up from the shape of the mold. From the collection of April and Bob Hill.

B. A square piece of stabilizer sandwich molded over a big round jug results in an unusual-looking bowl. From the collection of Chris and Kathy Shaker.

C. This delicate thread-web is made of cut-up artificial flowers and fuzzy chenille yarn molded over a bread-baking tin.

D. Not all forms must be round! Supplies to make flies for fishing cause these thread-web containers to sparkle.

cylinder vase with eyelash yarn

This project features a molded cylinder vase. The sparkle comes from a sprinkling of metallic fibers in the filler material called Krystal Flash, found in fly-fishing supply shops. You may substitute any metallic thread.

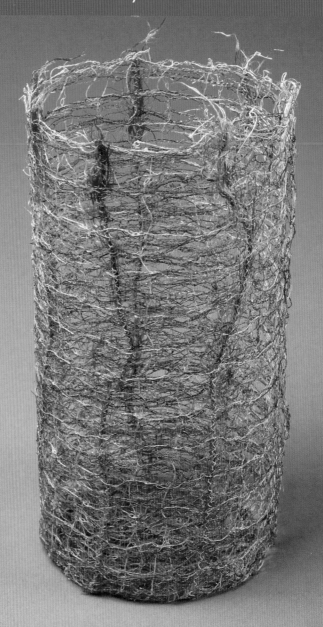

What You'll Need

- ☐ Cylinder vase for molding
- ☐ Black permanent pen
- ☐ Assorted filler materials: novelty eyelash yarn, metallic thread, or fly-fishing fiber supplies
- ☐ Water-soluble stabilizer
- ☐ Assorted spools of thread for sewing (recommend glossy finish, such as rayon or polyester)
- ☐ Basic supplies (see page 12)

How-Tos

Refer to the corresponding steps in Make a Molded Thread-Web Bowl (pages 14–17).

1. measure the form
Measure around the cylinder vase and multiply by 2. Measure the height of the vase from the rim to the center of the bottom of the vase. Add an extra inch in both directions.

 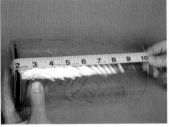

2. cut the stabilizer
Use the measurements from Step 1 to cut 2 rectangles of the water-soluble stabilizer. If necessary, use water-soluble thread to sew together two smaller pieces of stabilizer to make a big piece. Note: You don't need to make a template for this vase.

3. prepare the filler
Cut the eyelash yarn into lengths the same height as the rectangle measurement from Step 1 plus 3″. Cut enough strands to place side by side, 1″–2″ apart, across half of the rectangle. Cut the metallic thread or fly-fishing synthetic materials into a dozen or more lengths, each about 12″ long.

4. create the stabilizer sandwich
Fold a rectangle of stabilizer in half, and use a permanent pen to mark the halfway point on the top and bottom edges. Spread out this piece of stabilizer, and sprinkle the metallic strands over the stabilizer in a single layer. Use the metallic strands sparingly.

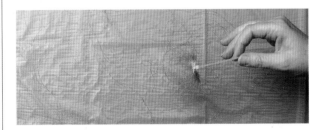

Place the eyelash yarn lengths vertically. Let the strands of yarn curve, wiggle, and sway, with the extra yarn going over the top edge of the stabilizer. Use an odd number of strands, placed every 1″–2″ apart over the left half of the stabilizer only. For a quick guide, place the stabilizer on a cutting mat. Align the edges of the stabilizer with the marked lines on the mat, and use the cutting lines to space out the vertical fibers. Cover with the second piece of stabilizer.

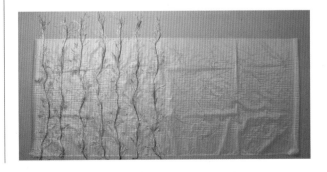

5. secure the sandwich
Connect the layers with evenly spaced columns of pins over the eyelash yarn and then with evenly spaced columns over the "blank" half of the stabilizer.

easy!

To make the wavy stitching lines, steer the stabilizer sandwich back and forth with your hands—similar to driving a car, with your hands at ten and two o'clock on the stabilizer. Allow the movement of your hands to control the distance between the curves relative to the speed of the "motor." Some sewing machines have a wavy line or serpentine decorative stitch that you can use. Consult the manual or sewing machine dealer to see if you have this stitch.

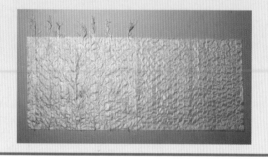

6. stitch a grid
Use a pale, blending thread color and a walking foot to stitch through the columns of pins. Use an open, narrow zigzag over the centers of the eyelash yarn and a wavy line through the rest of the pin columns. Add more wavy lines between the columns.

For this project, all the remaining stitching is horizontal. Use the same method as above to stitch parallel wavy lines from one side to the other side of the stabilizer. Start with the same pale thread to make the first set of parallel wavy lines. Next use another blending color to stitch wavy lines that cross the first layer of wavy lines. This is the basic grid for this vase.

7. add more stitching
Change to a regular sewing foot if desired. Continue to use a variety of solid colors, or select a variegated thread for the rest of the stitching. Keep stitching with the wavy lines, making sure the wavy lines cross each other as you stitch horizontally from side to side. Fold the excess eyelash yarn back on itself, and catch it in the wavy line stitching; this will reinforce the top edge. (Don't fret if some of the fibers of the yarn escape the stitching.)

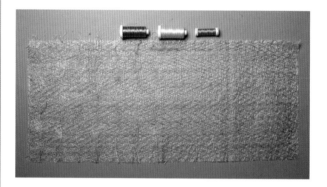

8. cut to size
Eliminate extra bulk on the bottom of the vase by trimming off a narrow strip of stabilizer sandwich on the plain side only. Determine how wide a strip to trim by rolling up the stabilizer sandwich on the vase and marking a point at the center bottom of the vase.

Unroll the stabilizer sandwich, and trim the excess web from the bottom edge. Start on the plain side, and stop at the marked midway point of the sandwich.

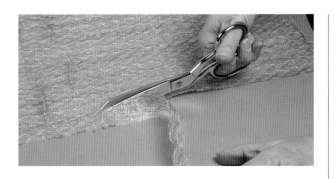

9. dissolve the stabilizer

10. mold the thread-web
With the right side down, spread the thread-web on the parchment paper. Tug at the thread-web to stretch it to its full size. Line up the vase along the plain end, with the top of the vase along the top edge of the thread-web.

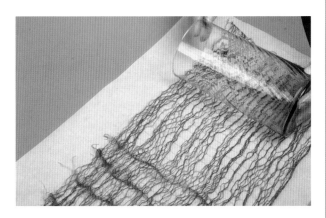

Roll up the thread-web onto the vase, making sure the web wraps snugly, with no air bubbles, and the top edge of the web and vase continue to line up. Continue to press the thread-web against the mold as you roll. Stop with the seam down.

Carefully press the thread-web ends onto the bottom of the vase, adjusting it to make it lay as flat as possible. If your hands stick to the thread-web, wet your hands or use a small piece of wet parchment paper to press against the web.

Cover the bottom of the thread-web with a piece of parchment paper. With the vase still on its side and with seam side down to keep the seam flat, push the end of the vase against the wall to begin to dry. Later, you may remove the parchment paper and turn the vase upside down to finish drying.

11. remove the dried thread-web

12. seal the finished vase

Variations

A. This is an extremely delicate thread-web vase. Instead of wrapping the web around the vase twice, the stabilizer sandwich was cut to size and stitched into a tube. After rinsing out the stabilizer, the wet thread-web was placed over the mold like a sock on a foot.

B. Recycled vinegar jars made a good mold for these vases. Silk twine and string placed in a grid are the only filler materials.

C. Cut-up artificial flowers and thread make up the dense filler materials for this vase. Multiple layers of free-motion loops and daisies in gradating colors of thread add to the depth of this glasslike thread-web vase.

D. This vase uses no filler materials at all! Instead, two different yarns were couched over one layer of Sulky Ultra Solvy, then stitched. The web had to be very delicate to fold in on itself and conform to the fluted glass vase mold.

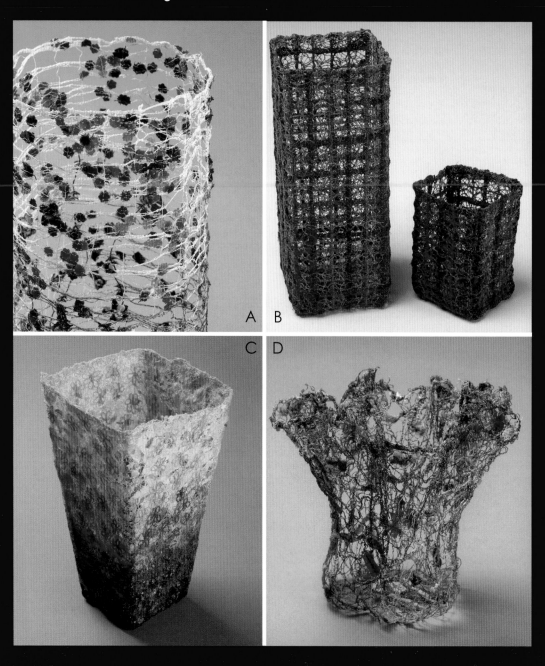

A B

C D

round bowl with
wavy sides

This fun little shaped bowl is a breeze to make. Cut scallops or wavy lines along the rim, and dry the bowl upside down, allowing the sides to ripple.

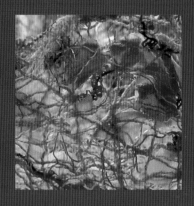

What You'll Need

- Support form for drying the bowl
- Water-soluble stabilizer, 2 square pieces about 2″ larger than the diameter of your template
- Assorted filler materials: thread, fabric snips (start with small pieces, about 2″ × 4″ each), silk artificial flowers, yarn
- Assorted spools of thread for sewing
- Basic supplies (see page 12)

How-Tos

Refer to the corresponding steps in Make a Shaped Thread-Web Bowl (pages 18–21).

1. make the template and cut the stabilizer

2. mark the cutting lines

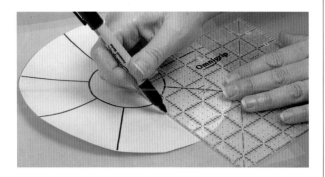

3. prepare the filler
Dismantle the artificial flowers, and discard the plastic parts. Set aside the leaves for another project. Cut apart the flower petals, then chop them into bits, ranging in size from ¼″ to ½″ across in any direction.

Without measuring, use a rotary cutter to cut the rectangles of fabrics into strips, and then into squares about ¼″ across in any direction.

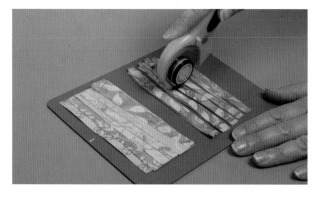

Cut the yarn into short lengths.

Line up the spools of thread. Unwind and cut 12″–24″ lengths to use in Step 4 when creating the stabilizer sandwich.

4. create the stabilizer sandwich

For this project, be sure to begin and end with the coils of thread.

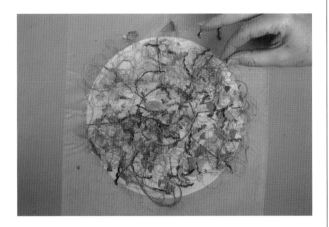

5. secure the sandwich

6. stitch a grid

7. add more stitching

Keep in mind that you will add more stitching after you shape the bowl (see Step 9).

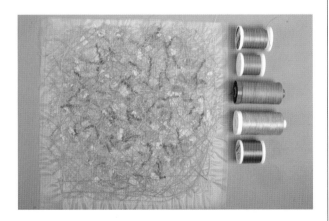

8. cut to size

9. shape the bowl
Overlap the cut edges about ¼″, and pin in place. Stitch along the cut edges from the rim to the center point and back again. Add more stitching to secure the shape.

Freehand cut wavy lines around the rim. Reinforce the cut edge with a few lines of stitching, or couch a piece of leftover yarn along the cut edge as I did. Use a blending thread color and an open but narrow zigzag to couch the yarn.

10. dissolve the stabilizer

11. let the shaped bowl dry
Place the right side of the wet thread-web on the support form. Let the sides dangle and form ripples. Fiddle with it to get a pleasing shape. Allow the bowl to dry thoroughly.

12. seal the finished bowl

Variations

A. This bowl was shaped with curved slits (instead of straight slits). Synthetic fluff and pearl braid cord from the fly-fishing shop really make this bowl sparkle.

B. This shallow bowl, with fabric snips for the filler material, features couched, variegated chenille in a lazy spiral from the rim to the center. From the collection of April and Bob Hill.

C. Both of these asymmetrical bowls were shaped by freehand cutting the slits at irregular intervals and depths. The smaller bowl has fabric snips and chenille yarn filler materials. The larger bowl uses clumps of raveled fabric edges and leftover thread snips for the filler materials. Large bowl created by Joan Metzger.

D. Triangle-shaped fabric snips give this bowl a jaunty style. From the collection of Sue McMahan.

bowl with motifs

You can incorporate motifs, or repeated design elements, in your thread-web containers. Look for ready-made motifs (such as leaves), design your own motifs, or cut out motifs from novelty or other fabrics.

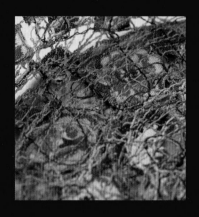

What You'll Need

- ☐ Support form for drying the bowl
- ☐ Water-soluble stabilizer, 2 square pieces about 2″ larger than the diameter of your template (1 piece each of Sulky Ultra Solvy and Sulky Super Solvy)
- ☐ Fabric with motifs
- ☐ Coordinating solid color fabrics: 4 different colors
- ☐ Assorted spools of thread for sewing
- ☐ Fusible web, such as Wonder Under
- ☐ Basic supplies (see page 12)

How-Tos

This shaped bowl uses a small floral motif clustered together on the bottom, with cut-up pieces of the motifs around the sides. Use a similar floral motif for your project or substitute another motif. Modify the directions as needed for your fabric choices.

The motifs can be clustered together, randomly placed, or carefully positioned to fall in specific areas of the finished bowl. The size of the motifs and how they might be placed together determine the size of the bowl.

Refer to the corresponding steps in Make a Shaped Thread-Web Bowl (pages 18–21).

1. make the template and cut the stabilizer

2. mark the cutting lines
For this bowl, use a grid ruler to draw a line ⅜″ from the marked line at the rim down to the end of the line, making a V shape. Repeat on both sides of every marked line to make 8 V-shaped wedges.

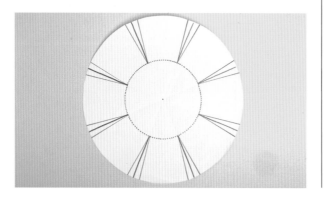

3. prepare the filler
Thread-web containers are seen from both sides, but most printed fabrics aren't reversible.

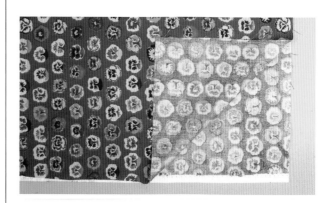

Make a printed fabric reversible by fusing another fabric to the wrong side of the print. Use a fusible web, such as Wonder Under, and follow the manufacturer's instructions to fuse the fabrics, wrong sides together. Fusing 2 fabrics together also reduces raveling, an additional benefit.

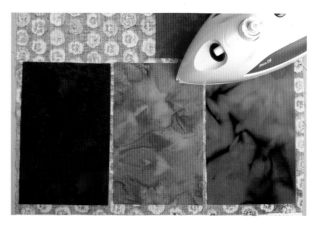

Cut motifs from 3 of the fabrics. Cut the fourth fabric into a rectangle about 3″ × 6″. Without measuring, use a rotary cutter to cut the rectangle into strips and then into squares about ¼″ across.

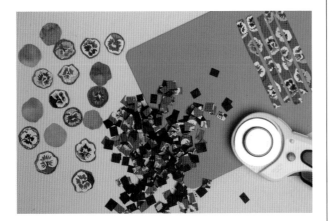

4. create the stabilizer sandwich

Center the heavier water-soluble stabilizer (Ultra Solvy) over the paper template. Tape the edges to the work surface. Use the template as a guide and cluster the whole motifs over the inner circle, with the flowers barely touching. Place the little squares around the sides at all angles, with the flower print side up most of the time. Occasionally turn a square over to show the solid color. Leave a space between the squares.

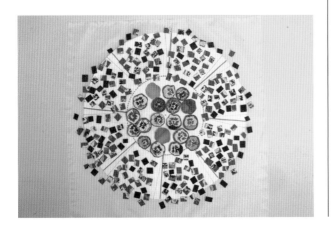

5. secure the sandwich

Use a glue stick or a hot iron on the steam setting to secure the layers together. (See tip on page 8 for the glue stick and steam ironing alternatives for securing the sandwich.)

6. stitch a grid

7. add more stitching

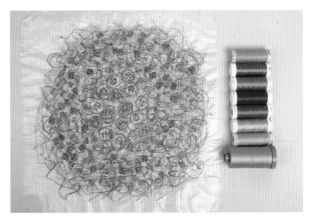

8. cut to size

Center and pin the paper template to the water-soluble stabilizer sandwich, adjusting the template so the inner circle is lined up with the clustered motifs. If needed, hold up the sandwich to a light source or use a light box to place the template. Cut out the circle. Next, cut out the 8 wedge shapes, cutting along the marked lines.

 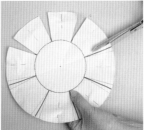

9. shape the bowl

Join the cut edges together by just slightly overlapping the cut edges and stitching along the edge from the rim to the center point.

Repeat this step with the remaining 7 wedges. The bowl is now brought up into shape. Add more stitching to secure the shape. Reinforce the rim with stitching, such as parallel lines, zigzagging, or serging.

10. dissolve the stabilizer

11. let the shaped bowl dry

The shaped bowl will probably need support while it dries. Try setting the thread-web bowl right side up with the form on the bottom of the bowl. Pull up on the sides. Often the weight of the support is enough to keep the sides upright without sagging.

If the sides do sag, place the bowl upside down over the form. Pull out the sides as much as possible—gravity will make them hang straight down.

If left to dry completely while upside down, the sides of the bowl will have ripples. About every 15 minutes, check to see if the bowl is stiff enough to dry right side up with the form in the middle of the thread-web bowl. By turning the bowl over, placing a weight in the middle, and stretching out the sides, you can ensure that the bowl will have fairly straight sides when dry.

12. seal the finished bowl

Variations

A. Fabric butterfly motifs are clustered closely together. The rim is left wild, with dangling and unruly threads.

B. Goldfish bowls and circle designs cut from one fabric are clustered together and stitched with one red-white-and-blue variegated thread.

C. Purchased artificial rubber tree leaves grace the sides of this delicate bowl with cut-up artificial flowers. The leaves were strategically placed to fall in between the wedge cuts used to shape the bowl.

D. Self-made little-girl motifs (also known as Button Babies) dance around this bowl. The hair, arms, and legs were added before the bowl was shaped. After shaping, scrunched green yarn was couched around the rim. Button faces were added after the bowl was sealed.

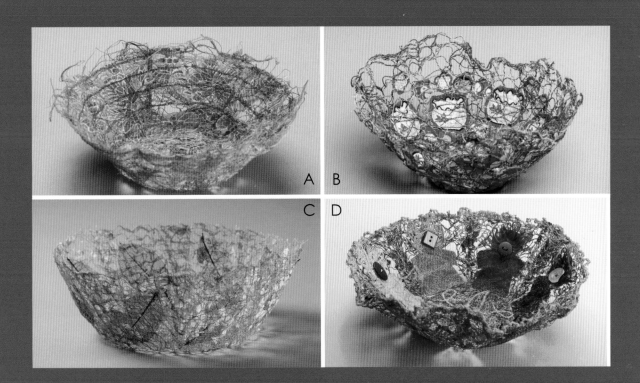

color bowls

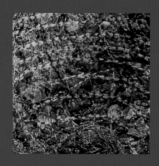

Filler materials may be used in a deliberate way to create colors and patterns. Instead of a random distribution of materials, use the filler materials and stitching to make a pattern or a new color.

What You'll Need

- ☐ Clean plastic dome-shaped coffee drink lid
- ☐ Juice can, 12 oz., empty and clean
- ☐ Water-soluble stabilizer, 2 square pieces about 2″ larger than the diameter of your template
- ☐ About 5 different, but closely related, solid or color-on-color patterned fabrics (each piece about 2″ × 4″)

- ☐ About 5 different, but closely related, solid colors of thread for filler materials
- ☐ Assorted spools of thread in similar colors for sewing
- ☐ Basic supplies (see page 12)

How-Tos

Refer to the corresponding steps in Make a Shaped Thread-Web Bowl (pages 18–21).

1. make the template and cut the stabilizer

Measure the coffee drink lid from rim to rim, running the tape measure over the middle of the lid.

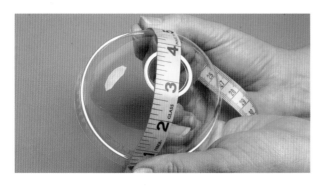

Make a paper template using this measurement. Use a compass to draw the circle or trace around the rim of a found plate or bowl with the same diameter. Center the juice can in the middle of the circle; trace around the rim. Cut 2 square pieces of water-soluble stabilizer about 2″ larger than the template.

2. mark the cutting lines

3. prepare the filler
Select about 5 different fabrics, closely related in color but ranging in value from medium-light to medium-dark.

Without measuring, use a rotary cutter to cut the rectangles of fabric into strips and then into squares about ¼″ across in any direction. Shuffle the fabric bits to see the new blended color. Add a little more of this or that to change the color, if desired. Get the spools of thread lined up or spool off several coils of thread, so they are ready to use in Step 4.

4. create the stabilizer sandwich

Begin and end with the coils of thread, with fabric snips placed between the coils of thread.

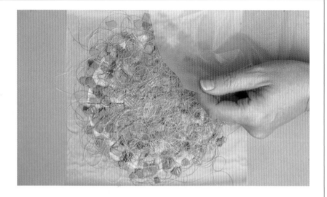

5. secure the sandwich

6. stitch a grid

7. add more stitching

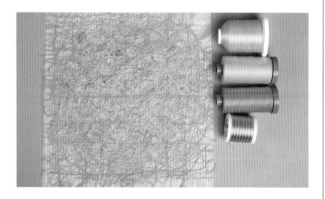

8. cut to size

9. shape the bowl

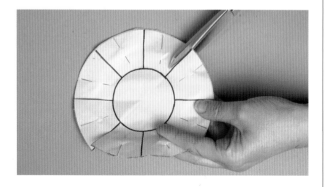

10. dissolve the stabilizer

11. let the shaped bowl dry

Spread the shaped bowl over the plastic coffee lid, centering the thread-web so the rim of the thread-web aligns with the edge of the lid. Gently push the center of the thread-web into the straw hole. From the outside, the web should conform smoothly to the lid with no puckers.

When completely dry, gently release the thread-web from the mold. If it is stuck, use a wooden skewer to loosen the thread-web so it will come off the lid.

12. seal the finished bowl

Variations

A. This set of three dishes started out as three finished flat pieces of stabilizer sandwiches. The designs were assembled using cut pieces of the "new" thread-web fabric. The shallow bowl was shaped, and the other two pieces were molded.

B. Molded over a square plate, this thread-web plaid is created from chenille and other specialty yarns. Vertical and horizontal stitching accent the plaid lines.

C. Leftover corner pieces from the set of color bowls make up this scrappy bowl. Minimal additional stitching holds the pieces together. Molded over the bottom of a big jug with a wild rim, this bowl looks much like a nest. From the collection of Christine and Paul Drumright.

D. Leftover thread, yarn, and fabric snips were mixed together to create this color bowl. This thread-web had to be very dense in order to push the web through the holes of the washer bowl (see page 9), creating the texture.

variations on a theme

Density

Density describes how much light passes through the finished thread-web. At one end of the density scale, an extremely delicate thread-web bowl is all stitching and no filler materials at all! At the other end of the scale, the filler materials and stitching make the thread-web appear almost solid.

Stitch Styles

The finished thread-web looks intricately criss-crossed, but each type of thread is actually stitched widely spaced (1˝–2˝ apart). The multiple layers of stitching with a variety of thread types result in the complex-looking thread-web. No special stitching skills are required!

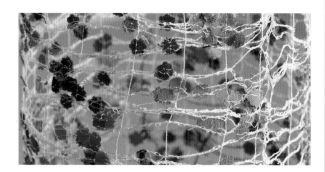

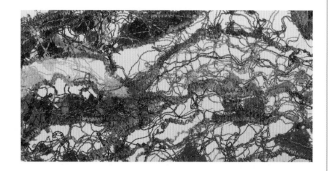

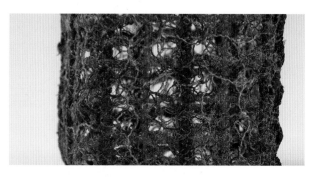

Once you've made one bowl, you'll want to make more. Using the same basic steps as described for making the shaped and molded bowls, try altering the density, stitch style, rims, and embellishments in your next thread-web creation.

Rims

The rims can be firmly finished, shaped, or wild. Let your imagination run wild—anything goes! For an extremely firm rim, the cut edge may be reinforced with additional stitching, using multiple rounds of straight stitching, zigzagging, or a serge-type stitch. For a firm but unfinished rim, leave the cut edge alone.

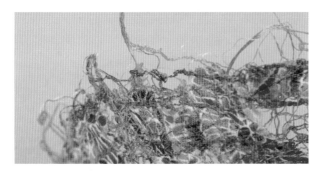

Embellishments

You may add all sorts of embellishments to the thread-web creation at any stage of the process.

Use machine or hand embroidery to add a design element to the thread-web before you rinse out the water-soluble stabilizer.

Made by Kathy Shaker.

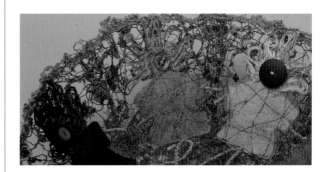

Oddly Shaped Molds

Are you wondering whether you can use an oddly shaped mold to make a thread-web container? Of course you can. Many odd shapes that are primarily symmetrical (square, triangular, hexagonal, or even fluted) work fine with a round template. Fit the thread-web over the mold as directed for round forms. Simply measure from rim to rim over the widest part (usually the center). Use this measurement as the diameter when drawing the circle template.

For other shapes, think about how you might form or wrap the wet thread-web onto the shape. Here are some examples.

Both the long oval olive dish and the flattened oval vase are most closely related to a rectangle. For the olive dish, measure rim to rim along the widest part of the olive dish and along the length. For the vase, measure around the vase and the height, including the bottom. For both, add an extra inch or two before making the stabilizer sandwich. Trim down as needed before molding the thread-web.

Made by Susan Howell.

With vases that are wider at the bottom and narrower at the top, the dried thread-web can't slide off, so you have to work around this.

One way is to mold the thread-web in two or more sections, then put the sections together.

The thread-web is molded in two halves.

Overlap the edges to put the two halves back together.

Another possibility is to form the thread-web over the mold and cut it partially or completely off. These solutions pose challenges to solve, such as how to put the container back together again. Try positioning the sections with the edges slightly overlapped, so it will hold together.

The thread-web is molded in two halves.

Overlap the edges to put the two halves back together.

Another possibility is to hand sew the sections together with a curved needle (found in fabric stores) or a flexible needle (found in bead shops) with monofilament or contrasting thread colors.

This thread-web was slit enough to slide off the mold, then sewn back together.

Unlimited Possibilities

Now that you know all the thread-web basics, you can use the projects as a starting point for your own thread-web creations. Try different combinations of filler materials. Use different densities, stitch styles, rims, and embellishments according to your own imagination.

And come to think of it, why limit yourself to bowls and vases? Consider other ways to use thread-web:

☐ Layer thread-web on quilts and garments for texture and color, or make a garment just of thread-web.

☐ Make sheets of thread-web and use like paper in scrapbooks, collages, altered books, and multimedia art projects.

☐ Sculpt thread-web like paper pulp.

☐ Make a thread-web hat.

☐ Make a lampshade with Mylar, and cover it with thread-web.

☐ You can even make an entire quilt from thread.

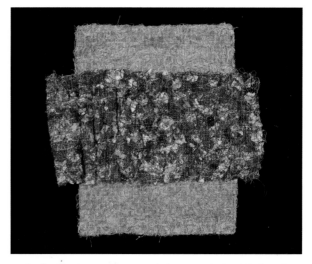

Surface Tension, a quilt created almost entirely with thread; photograph by Craig Howell, Bend, Oregon

About the Author

From a very early age, Wendy remembers dreaming of colors. Her first sewing projects were doll quilts and clothing. In high school, when her sewing teacher insisted it couldn't be done, Wendy made a faux fur coat with perfect bound buttonholes to prove that it could. Creative work with fabrics and fibers, by both hand and machine, has been a steady force in Wendy's life.

Wendy's work has been in print in some form since 1992. She has written magazine articles, contributed projects to several books, and has authored two other books: *On the Surface; Thread Embellishment & Fabric Manipulation* and *Two-for-One Foundation Piecing; Reversible Quilts and More*, both with C&T Publishing.

Wendy lives in Sunriver, Oregon. Her local quilt guild recently awarded her the title of Master Quilter, made all the more meaningful because it came from her community members.

Resources

American & Efird
American & Efird offers threads for quilting, home decor, apparel, embroidery, and general crafts applications under Mettler, Signature, and Maxi-Lock brands. Their products are available online and in retail stores.

800-847-3235

www.amefird.com (product information and lists of distributors and Internet retailers)

consumer.homepage@amefird.com

Aurifil (available through Huckleberry Quiltworks)
Huckleberry Quiltworks stocks the entire Aurifil cotton color line, in both spools and cones, in 28, 40, and 50 weights. They carry a full line of Aurilux, a 36-weight polyester thread for quilting, embroidery, and garment construction. They also carry a 12-weight wool in an assortment of colors for hand or machine work.

406-837-2941, 866-577- 8458

www.lovetoquilt.com (wholesale and retail sales)

Coats & Clark
Coats & Clark offers a full range of products for sewing, quilting, knitting, crochet, and machine and hand embroidery. Their products are available online and in retail stores.

800-648-1479

www.coatsandclark.com (product information and links to retail outlets)

Gütermann
Gütermann has a wide range of threads: cotton and polyester, for hand and machine sewing, and specialty threads, including upholstery, rayon embroidery, metallic, bobbin, fusible, invisible, elastic, and silk. Gütermann also makes beads in assorted styles and colors. Their products are available online and in retail stores.

www.gutermann.com (product information)

Madeira
Madeira makes embroidery threads and supplies, including rayon, polyester, metallic, holographic, and Lana wool. Their products are available online and in retail stores, including:

Nancy's Notions

800-833-0690

www.nancysnotions.com (retail sales)

www.madeira.com (product information)

Sulky of America
Sulky provides a wide range of threads, stabilizers, books, and other products. Products are available online and in retail stores including:

Speed Stitch, Inc.

866-829-7235

www.speedstitch.com (retail sales)

info@speedstitch.com

www.sulky.com (product information and list of retail outlets)

YLI Corp.
YLI manufactures decorative threads, serger threads, silk ribbon, quilting threads, and bobbin threads, including Pearl Crown Rayon, Candlelight, Wonder Invisible, Soft Touch, Machine Quilting, and Select. Products are available online and in retail stores

www.ylicorp.com (information, online orders, lists of distributors and retail outlets)

Cotton Patch Mail Order
Fabric, thread, and quilting supplies
3405 Hall Lane, Dept. CTB
Lafayette, CA 94549
800-835-4418
email: quiltusa@yahoo.com
www.quiltusa.com

For more information
Ask for a free catalog:
C&T Publishing, Inc.
P.O. Box 1456
Lafayette, CA 94549
800-284-1114
email: ctinfo@ctpub.com
www.ctpub.com